Intermediate 2

French

© Scottish Qualifications Authority
All rights reserved. Copying prohibited. No part of this publication may be reproduced, stored in a retrieval system, or
transmitted in any form or by any means, electronic, mechanical, photocopying, recording or otherwise.

First exam published in 2005.
Published by Leckie & Leckie Ltd, 3rd Floor, 4 Queen Street, Edinburgh EH2 1JE
tel: 0131 220 6831 fax: 0131 225 9987 enquiries@leckieandleckie.co.uk www.leckieandleckie.co.uk

ISBN 978-1-84372-660-9

A CIP Catalogue record for this book is available from the British Library.

Leckie & Leckie is a division of Huveaux plc.

Leckie & Leckie is grateful to the copyright holders, as credited at the back of the book, for permission to use their material.
Every effort has been made to trace the copyright holders and to obtain their permission for the use of copyright material.
Leckie & Leckie will gladly receive information enabling them to rectify any error or omission in subsequent editions.

[BLANK PAGE]

FOR OFFICIAL USE

Mark [ ]

X059/201

NATIONAL QUALIFICATIONS 2005	TUESDAY, 17 MAY 9.00 AM – 10.10 AM	**FRENCH INTERMEDIATE 2** Reading

---

Fill in these boxes and read what is printed below.

Full name of centre

[ ]

Town

[ ]

Forename(s)

[ ]

Surname

[ ]

Date of birth
Day Month Year

[ ][ ][ ][ ][ ][ ]

Scottish candidate number

[ ][ ][ ][ ][ ][ ][ ][ ][ ]

Number of seat

[ ]

When you are told to do so, open your paper and write your answers **in English** in the spaces provided.

You may use a French dictionary.

Before leaving the examination room you must give this book to the invigilator. If you do not, you may lose all the marks for this paper.

SCOTTISH
QUALIFICATIONS
AUTHORITY

©

DO NOT
WRITE IN
THIS
MARGIN

Points

1. You are interested in a study programme called <<Connaissance de la France>> and you visit this website.

Connaissance de la France

Les stages <<Connaissance de la France>> permettent à des jeunes français et à des jeunes étrangers de passer un séjour de huit à quinze jours dans une région de la France.

Avant de partir pour la province, on visite la capitale et on passe deux nuits à Paris avec pension complète (petit déjeuner, déjeuner, dîner).

Départ de Paris le soir du troisième jour pour un voyage en wagon "couchette" vers la région choisie.

Les demandes de renseignements complémentaires s'effectuent auprès de l'Ambassade de France.

(a) For which **two** groups of people is <<Connaissance de la France>> intended?

1

_____

(b) How long does a visit to a region last?

1

_____

(c) What is included in your stay in Paris?

1

_____

(d) When do you leave Paris?

1

_____

(e) Where can you get further details?

1

_____

Points

2. You decide to visit the region of Champagne Ardennes. This website gives you further information about your stay.

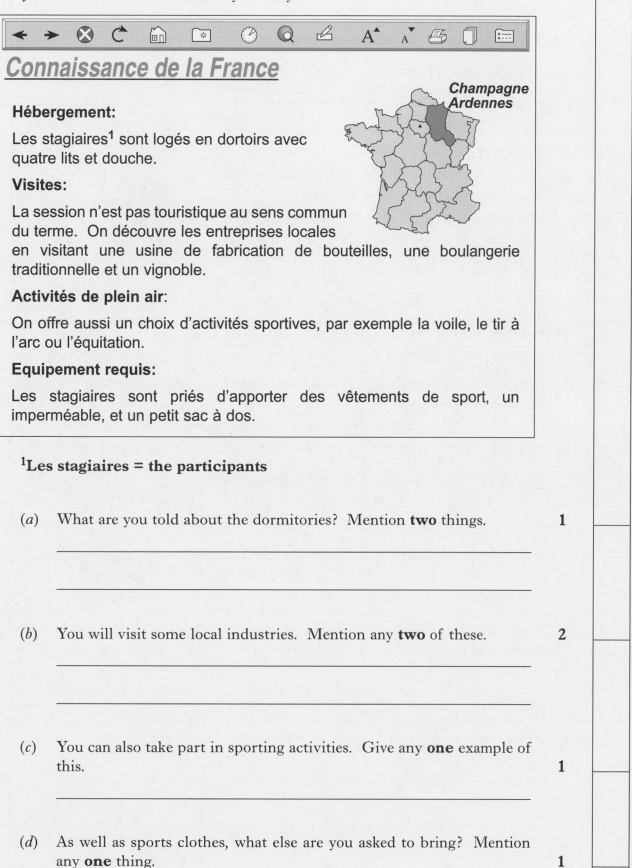

Connaissance de la France

Champagne
Ardennes

Hébergement:

Les stagiaires[1] sont logés en dortoirs avec quatre lits et douche.

Visites:

La session n'est pas touristique au sens commun du terme. On découvre les entreprises locales en visitant une usine de fabrication de bouteilles, une boulangerie traditionnelle et un vignoble.

Activités de plein air:

On offre aussi un choix d'activités sportives, par exemple la voile, le tir à l'arc ou l'équitation.

Equipement requis:

Les stagiaires sont priés d'apporter des vêtements de sport, un imperméable, et un petit sac à dos.

[1]**Les stagiaires = the participants**

(a) What are you told about the dormitories? Mention **two** things.

_____

_____

1

(b) You will visit some local industries. Mention any **two** of these.

_____

_____

2

(c) You can also take part in sporting activities. Give any **one** example of this.

_____

1

(d) As well as sports clothes, what else are you asked to bring? Mention any **one** thing.

_____

1

Points

3. During your stay in France you read this article in a magazine.

Activité physique et alimentation

Le député[1] Jean-Marie Le Guen veut limiter la publicité des sucreries et des boissons gazeuses à la télévision car le nombre de jeunes obèses[2] a doublé en France. Plus les jeunes regardent la télé ou jouent avec les ordinateurs plus ils grossissent.

Par contre pratiquer régulièrement un sport contribue à la bonne santé et développe l'esprit d'équipe.

Si tu ne t'intéresses pas au sport, il est important quand même d'augmenter le temps d'activité. Pourquoi ne pas te rendre à pied à l'école?

---

[1]**le député = a member of parliament**
[2]**obèse = obese, very fat**

(a) Which sort of TV advertising does Jean-Marie Le Guen wish to limit? Mention any **one** thing.

    1

_____

(b) Why does he want to introduce these changes?

    1

_____

(c) Which **two** leisure activities are blamed for this trend in young people?

    1

_____

(d) Apart from improving your health, which other benefit of taking up sports is mentioned?

    1

_____

(e) If you are not interested in sport, how else can you increase your level of activity?

    1

_____

[Turn over for Question 4 on *Page six*

4. You read another article in the magazine.

Comment dépensez-vous votre argent?

A l'époque de nos grands-parents, parler d'argent était impoli et vulgaire. Mais aujourd'hui ce n'est plus un problème.

Selon une enquête, 62% des jeunes déclarent que l'argent c'est pour s'acheter des choses qui font plaisir. Mais, pour les adultes, les dépenses sont consacrées à la maison ou à la voiture.

Sophie, 15 ans

Mes parents sont séparés et ma mère me donne deux cent cinquante euros par mois. Avec ça, je dois gérer[1] mes dépenses de tous les jours: vêtements, chaussures et collants. Elle refuse de me payer le coiffeur parce que je me fais des coupes excentriques et une fois je suis rentrée avec les cheveux pourpres.

Mon père me paie les loisirs et les sorties avec les copains. Si je veux avoir plus d'argent je dois le justifier et négocier. J'ai même utilisé une forme de chantage[2] pour obtenir l'objet de mes rêves. C'est-à-dire: si je réussis à mes examens, mon père m'a promis une console de jeux.

Mes tantes, mes oncles et mes grands-parents m'offrent toujours de l'argent à mon anniversaire et à Noël. Avec ça, je dois payer les frais de mon portable.

Nicolas, 23 ans

Selon moi, l'argent n'a pas de valeur, sauf qu'on le gagne en travaillant. A l'âge de onze ans, je livrais des journaux. Et j'avais déjà un compte en banque où je mettais chaque semaine l'argent que j'avais gagné. J'étais content quand je pouvais offrir des petits cadeaux à mes parents parce que ça m'a donné un goût de liberté.

Maintenant j'habite loin de chez moi parce que je fais actuellement mes études à l'université de Montpellier pour être médecin. Pour m'aider, mes parents me donnent une bourse[3] qui me paie le matériel éducatif et le logement. Mais pour gagner un peu d'argent supplémentaire, j'organise aussi les boums pour enfants le samedi, ce qui me rapporte un peu moins de trois cents euros par mois. J'économise cent euros pour partir en vacances aux Etats-Unis avec des amis l'été prochain.

[1]gérer = organise, manage
[2]le chantage = blackmail
[3]une bourse = a grant

Points

4. (continued)

(*a*)   What does the title question of the article ask?   1

_____

(*b*)   According to the survey:

  (i) what do young people spend money on?   1

  _____

  (ii) what do adults spend money on? Mention **two** things.   1

  _____

  _____

Sophie

(*c*)   How does Sophie spend the money she gets from her mother?   1

_____

(*d*)   Why does her mother refuse to pay for Sophie's visits to the
       hairdresser?   1

_____

(*e*)   What does the money from her father pay for?   1

_____

(*f*)   What does Sophie mean when she says she has "blackmailed" her
       father?   2

_____

_____

(*g*)   What does she do with her birthday money?   1

_____

[Turn over for Question 4(*h*)–(*l*) on *Page eight*

Points

4. **(continued)**

Nicolas

(*h*)   According to Nicolas, when does money only have true value?   1

_____

(*i*)   (i)   How did he get money at the age of 11?   1

_____

(ii)   What did he do with his money? Mention any **one** thing.   1

_____

(*j*)   Now he is a student, what do his parents pay for? Mention any **one** thing.   1

_____

(*k*)   How does he earn extra money?   1

_____

(*l*)   What does he intend to do with the money he is saving?   1

_____

Total (30 points)

= 30 marks

[END OF QUESTION PAPER]

X059/203

NATIONAL
QUALIFICATIONS
2005

TUESDAY, 17 MAY
10.30 AM – 11.00 AM

FRENCH
INTERMEDIATE 2
Listening Transcript

This paper must not be seen by any candidate.

The material overleaf is provided for use in an emergency only (eg the recording or equipment proving faulty) or where permission has been given in advance by SQA for the material to be read to candidates with special needs. The material must be read exactly as printed.

SCOTTISH
QUALIFICATIONS
AUTHORITY

©

> **Instructions to reader(s):**
>
> For each item, read the English **once**, then read the French **twice**, with an interval of 1 minute between the two readings. On completion of the second reading, pause for the length of time indicated in brackets after each item, to allow the candidates to write their answers.
>
> Where special arrangements have been agreed in advance to allow the reading of the material, those sections marked **(f)** should be read by a female speaker and those marked **(m)** by a male: those sections marked **(t)** should be read by the teacher.

(t) You are taking part in a study programme in France.

Question number one.

While you are visiting a vineyard a young student, Isabelle, tells you about her work.

(f)
Je suis étudiante en géographie et ça fait trois ans que je fais du travail saisonnier. Beaucoup de mes amis travaillent dans des bureaux ou des hôtels. Moi, je préfère travailler à la campagne parce qu'on est toujours au grand air.

On reçoit mille euros par mois et le logement et la nourriture sont compris.

Normalement chacun prépare son propre petit déjeuner—une tasse de café avec du pain ou des céréales. Et à 10 heures précises, on nous apporte un sandwich au saucisson ou au fromage. Puis à midi on a une coupure de deux heures et demie pour déjeuner, car il fait souvent trop chaud pour travailler.

C'est la femme du vigneron qui nous prépare le déjeuner et le dîner et c'est toujours un repas délicieux.

(3 minutes)

(t) **Question number two.**

Isabelle goes on to talk about how she would like to improve her home town.

(f)
Quand j'aurai fini mes études, j'ai l'intention de retourner à ma ville natale. C'est une belle ville . . . très vieille . . . avec des quartiers historiques.

Mais maintenant il y a aussi beaucoup de nouvelles banlieues, beaucoup de circulation et, à cause de ça, des problèmes de pollution. Je crois que la solution c'est d'améliorer le système de transports en commun: c'est-à-dire encourager les autobus et décourager les voitures.

Je voudrais aussi améliorer la vie des jeunes. Je voudrais construire un grand complexe sportif et je voudrais que les écoles ferment tous les jours à deux heures de l'après-midi. Comme ça les jeunes auraient plus de temps pour découvrir les sports.

(3 minutes)

(t)   Question number three.

On the radio you hear about Henri, a young boy who went missing in the Alps, but who has been found safe and sound.

(m)   C'est un miracle: Henri a finalement été retrouvé, sain et sauf à sept heures ce matin. Ce garçon de treize ans qui vient de Paris avait disparu hier samedi alors qu'il skiait seul pendant ses vacances en montagne. Ses parents se sont inquiétés quand Henri n'est pas arrivé à leur point de rendez-vous fixé.

Les gendarmes ont cherché le garçon pendant la nuit à l'aide de deux hélicoptères de la protection civile. Heureusement, Henri était équipé d'une casquette en laine et de vêtements chauds car il fait très froid la nuit dans la montagne.

Quand les gendarmes ont trouvé Henri il dormait tranquillement au pied d'un arbre. A leur grande surprise il avait réussi à marcher plus d'une dizaine de kilomètres malgré le brouillard et un bras cassé.

(3 minutes)

(t)   End of test.

Now look over your answers.

[END OF TRANSCRIPT]

[BLANK PAGE]

FOR OFFICIAL USE

Mark

X059/202

NATIONAL
QUALIFICATIONS
2005

TUESDAY, 17 MAY
10.30 AM – 11.00 AM

FRENCH
INTERMEDIATE 2
Listening

Fill in these boxes and read what is printed below.

Full name of centre

Town

Forename(s)

Surname

Date of birth
Day Month Year

Scottish candidate number

Number of seat

When you are told to do so, open your paper.

You will hear three items in French. You will hear each item twice, with an interval of one minute between playings, then you will have time to answer the questions about it before hearing the next item.

Write your answers, **in English**, in this book, in the appropriate spaces.

You may take notes as you are listening to the French, but only in this paper.

You may **not** use a French dictionary.

You are not allowed to leave the examination room until the end of the test.

Before leaving the examination room you must give this book to the invigilator. If you do not, you may lose all the marks for this paper.

SCOTTISH
QUALIFICATIONS
AUTHORITY

©

Points

You are taking part in a study programme in France.

1. While you are visiting a vineyard a young student, Isabelle, tells you about her work.

   (*a*) Which subject is Isabelle studying?   **1**

   _____

   (*b*) For how long has Isabelle been doing seasonal work?   **1**

   _____

   (*c*) Isabelle tells you about the kind of work her friends do. Where do they work? Mention any **one** place.   **1**

   _____

   (*d*) How much does Isabelle earn?   **1**

   _____

   (*e*) Which other **two** benefits does her work include?   **1**

   _____

   _____

   (*f*) What are the arrangements for breakfast? Mention **one** thing.   **1**

   _____

   (*g*) (i) How long is the lunch break?   **1**

   _____

   (ii) Why is it so long?   **1**

   _____

   *   *   *   *   *

Points

DO NOT
WRITE IN
THIS
MARGIN

2. Isabelle goes on to talk about how she would like to improve her home town.

(*a*) She says her home town is beautiful. What else does she say about it?
Mention any **one** thing.

1

_____

(*b*) How has the town changed? Mention any **two** things.

2

_____

_____

(*c*) What is Isabelle's plan to improve the situation?

1

_____

(*d*) What does Isabelle want to build to improve life for young people?

1

_____

(*e*) Why does she want schools to close at 2 pm each day?

1

_____

*   *   *   *   *

[Turn over for Question 3 on *Page four*

Points

3. On the radio you hear about Henri, a young boy who went missing in the Alps, but who has been found safe and sound.

(*a*) When was Henri found?

   1

_____

(*b*) What was he doing when he disappeared?

   1

_____

(*c*) When did his parents start to worry?

   1

_____

(*d*) What clothing was Henri wearing? Mention any **one** thing.

   1

_____

(*e*) The police were surprised at how far Henri had walked. Give **two** reasons why they were surprised.

   2

_____

_____

*   *   *   *   *

**Total (20 Points)
= 20 marks**

[END OF QUESTION PAPER]

X059/204

NATIONAL
QUALIFICATIONS
2005

TUESDAY, 17 MAY
11.20 AM – 12.00 NOON

FRENCH
INTERMEDIATE 2
Writing

20 marks are allocated to this paper.

You may use a French dictionary.

SCOTTISH
QUALIFICATIONS
AUTHORITY

You are preparing an application for the job advertised below.

Vous voulez travailler en France cet été?
Village Vacances (160 lits) recrute

- Serveurs/Serveuses de restaurant

  et

- Femmes/Hommes de ménage

Conditions : 35h/semaine, possibilité logement.

Etudiants/Etudiantes accepté(e)s

Envoyer CV + lettre à

Mme E. CHARBONNIER

127 rue de Jarnac

16170 Rouillac

FRANCE

To help you to write your application, you have been given the following checklist of information to give about yourself and to ask about the job:

- name, age, where you live
- leisure interests
- school/college career – subjects studied previously/being studied now
- reasons for application
- request for information about the job.

Make sure you deal with **all** of these points. You could also include the following information:

- any previous links with France or a French-speaking country
- work experience, if any.

You have also been given a way to start and finish this formal type of letter:

Formal opening to letter of application

Monsieur/Madame/Messieurs,

Suite à votre annonce, je me permets de poser ma candidature pour le poste de . . .

Formal finish to letter of application

En espérant que ma demande retiendra votre attention, je vous prie d'accepter, Monsieur/Madame/Messieurs, l'expression de mes sentiments distingués.

Use all of this to help prepare the letter and then copy out your finished version. You should write 120–150 words, excluding the formal phrases you have been given. You may use a French dictionary.

[END OF QUESTION PAPER]

[BLANK PAGE]

FOR OFFICIAL USE

Mark

X059/201

NATIONAL
QUALIFICATIONS
2006

TUESDAY, 16 MAY
9.00 AM – 10.10 AM

FRENCH
INTERMEDIATE 2
Reading

Fill in these boxes and read what is printed below.

Full name of centre

Town

Forename(s)

Surname

Date of birth
Day Month Year   Scottish candidate number   Number of seat

When you are told to do so, open your paper and write your answers **in English** in the spaces provided.

You may use a French dictionary.

Before leaving the examination room you must give this book to the invigilator. If you do not, you may lose all the marks for this paper.

SCOTTISH
QUALIFICATIONS
AUTHORITY

Points

You are very interested in Canada and would like to go there. You look on the Internet for some information.

1. You read a website describing a project in Canada.

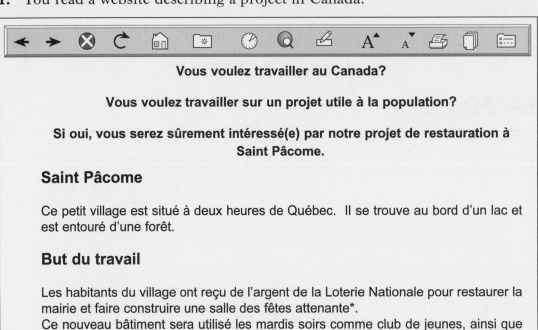

Vous voulez travailler au Canada?

Vous voulez travailler sur un projet utile à la population?

Si oui, vous serez sûrement intéressé(e) par notre projet de restauration à Saint Pâcome.

Saint Pâcome

Ce petit village est situé à deux heures de Québec. Il se trouve au bord d'un lac et est entouré d'une forêt.

But du travail

Les habitants du village ont reçu de l'argent de la Loterie Nationale pour restaurer la mairie et faire construire une salle des fêtes attenante*.
Ce nouveau bâtiment sera utilisé les mardis soirs comme club de jeunes, ainsi que pour célébrer des mariages.

*attenante = attached

(a) According to the first two questions, what type of person would be interested in this project?

Tick (✓) **one** box.

1

Someone who wants to travel around Canada	
Someone who wants to work in Canada	
Someone who is studying the population of Canada	

(b) Where are we told the village is? Mention any **two** things.

2

_____

_____

(c) What does the project involve? Mention any **one** thing.

1

_____

(d) What will the new building be used for? Mention any **one** thing.

1

_____

DO NOT WRITE IN THIS MARGIN

Points

2. Having sent an e-mail asking for more information, you receive a reply from Jean-Claude, one of the project leaders.

10/03/2006 16:22

From: Jean-Claude

Subject: Canada

Voici plus de détails qui répondront à vos questions.

Le transport / le logement
Les frais de transport et de logement seront payés par notre organisation. Vous serez nourri et logé chez une famille d'accueil.

Les affaires personnelles
Au mois de juillet il fait très chaud ici, alors apportez des vêtements légers et n'oubliez pas votre crème solaire.

Votre temps libre
Pendant votre temps libre, vous pouvez profiter des sports aquatiques offerts sur le lac comme la planche à voile, le ski nautique ou la pêche.

Veuillez m'envoyer un e-mail avec les détails de votre voyage. Comme ça je viendrai vous chercher à l'aéroport.

A bientôt
Jean-Claude

(*a*) Where will you stay?

1

_____

(*b*) What personal items are you told to bring with you? Mention any **one** thing.

1

_____

(*c*) Which water sports could you do in your free-time? Mention any **two**.

2

_____

_____

(*d*) Why does Jean-Claude want details of your travel arrangements?

1

_____

[Turn over

Points

3. While working in Canada you read a magazine article in which two young people give their views on life in the country.

Adrien – 20 ans

Depuis cinq ans j'étudie en ville mais je préfère la campagne car mes loisirs favoris sont le cyclisme et les randonnées. Plus tard je veux vivre à la campagne pour y élever mes enfants dans un environnement tranquille et sûr.

Dorothée – 15 ans

Je n'ai qu'une envie: quitter le village où je vis. C'est ennuyeux ici car il n'y a rien à faire et tous les magasins ferment tôt. Alors, beaucoup de jeunes quittent notre village pour aller dans les grandes villes et y chercher du travail.

Adrien

(a) How long has Adrien been studying in town?   **1**

_____

(b) Why does he want to live in the country later? Mention any **one** thing.   **1**

_____

Dorothée

(c) What does Dorothée find boring about her village?   **2**

_____

_____

(d) Why do young people move to the big towns, according to Dorothée?   **1**

_____

[Turn over for Question 4 on *Pages six, seven* and *eight*

4. You then read an article about an association for sick children.

Nous réalisons des rêves !

Notre association

Notre but est de réaliser les rêves des enfants malades. Pour beaucoup d'enfants leur rêve est de visiter un parc d'attractions, de nager avec les dauphins ou de rencontrer des personnalités du monde sportif ou de la télévision.

Voici les expériences de deux jeunes que nous avons pu aider.

Amélie, 16 ans

J'ai toujours voulu aller sur le plateau[1] de ma série favorite et rencontrer les acteurs et actrices que je vois à la télé chaque semaine. Un soir de février dernier j'ai reçu un coup de téléphone que je n'oublierai jamais. Le résultat? J'ai pu réaliser mon rêve et aller visiter le studio. J'ai passé quinze jours en Californie dans un grand hôtel face à l'Océan Pacifique.

Ma première surprise: Sur le plateau tout le monde était très gentil! Ces célèbres acteurs et actrices me disaient bonjour, à moi!

En début d'après-midi, le metteur en scène[2] a décidé de me faire jouer dans la série. Quel choc! Au début j'ai refusé. Je suis tellement timide que je n'osais pas. Mais le metteur en scène m'a persuadée et j'ai donc joué le rôle d'une infirmière.

Christophe, 15 ans

Ma passion c'est la musique. J'apprends à jouer du piano depuis cinq ans et chaque week-end je joue de la batterie avec des amis. Mon rêve était de rencontrer mon groupe préféré quand ils visitaient ma ville. Malheureusement je n'ai pas pu assister à leur concert car j'étais à l'hôpital pendant un mois. Mais le groupe est venu me rendre visite! On a même joué ensemble et c'est un des meilleurs moments de ma vie.

Comment nous aider?

Vouz pouvez participer financièrement. En moyenne, chaque projet coûte 800 euros. Cette somme comprend les frais de transport, d'hébergement et de nourriture pour l'enfant et un accompagnateur.

Vouz pouvez aussi inviter les enfants à passer quelques jours chez vous à visiter les endroits intéressants de votre quartier.

Vous pouvez également aider les enfants hospitalisés à continuer à étudier avec la lecture, par exemple.

Vous n'oublierez jamais le sourire et la joie des enfants.

[1]le plateau = set
[2]le metteur en scène = director

Points

4. (continued)

(a) This association makes dreams come true for sick children. Mention any **two** "dreams" that many children have.

2

_____

_____

Amélie

(b) What was Amélie's dream? Mention any **one** thing.

1

_____

(c) What does Amélie say about her stay in California? Mention any **one** thing.

1

_____

(d) What surprised her when she arrived at the studio? Mention any **one** thing.

1

_____

(e) The director offered her a part in the show.

 (i) Why did she refuse at first?

1

_____

 (ii) What role did she eventually play?

1

_____

Christophe

(f) What shows that Christophe is keen on music? Mention **two** things.

2

_____

_____

(g) What was Christophe's dream?

1

_____

Points

4. (continued)

(*h*)   How did his dream eventually come true? Mention any **one** thing.   **1**

_____

(*i*)   You can help the association by giving money.

   (i) What exactly does the money pay for? Mention **two** things.   **1**

    _____

    _____

   (ii) Who does the money pay for?   **1**

    _____

(*j*)   In which other ways can you help? Mention any **two** things.   **2**

_____

_____

Total (30 points)

= 30 marks

[END OF QUESTION PAPER]

X059/203

NATIONAL
QUALIFICATIONS
2006

TUESDAY, 16 MAY
10.30 AM – 11.00 AM

FRENCH
INTERMEDIATE 2
Listening Transcript

This paper must not be seen by any candidate.

The material overleaf is provided for use in an emergency only (eg the recording or equipment proving faulty) or where permission has been given in advance by SQA for the material to be read to candidates with additional support needs. The material must be read exactly as printed.

SCOTTISH
QUALIFICATIONS
AUTHORITY

©

> **Instructions to reader(s):**
>
> For each item, read the English **once**, then read the French **twice**, with an interval of 1 minute between the two readings. On completion of the second reading, pause for the length of time indicated in brackets after each item, to allow the candidates to write their answers.
>
> Where special arrangements have been agreed in advance to allow the reading of the material, those sections marked **(f)** should be read by a female speaker and those marked **(m)** by a male: those sections marked **(t)** should be read by the teacher.

(t) You are working on a building project in Canada.

Question number one.

Céline, one of the other participants, tells you about her home and school life in the North of Canada.

(f) **Salut, je m'appelle Céline et j'habite au nord du Canada. Comme le collège le plus près se trouve à 60 km de chez moi, je fais mes études à la maison par Internet. Les cours commencent à 8 heures du matin, alors je me lève vers 7 heures et je prends le petit déjeuner vers 7 heures et demie avec ma famille, c'est-à-dire mes deux soeurs et mes parents. Normalement je commence la journée avec un cours d'espagnol ou d'anglais. J'adore les langues étrangères et elles sont importantes pour moi car je veux être journaliste plus tard. Les cours finissent à 13 heures et l'après-midi je dois aider ma mère à faire le ménage. Tous les jours, je fais la vaisselle, passe l'aspirateur et nettoie ma chambre. J'aime suivre les cours par Internet car je peux travailler à mon rythme. Le seul inconvénient est que je n'ai pas de camarades de classe avec qui je peux discuter.**

(3 minutes)

(t) Question number two.

Céline then goes on to tell you about a visit she made to Scotland.

(f) **Quand j'avais 16 ans, j'ai visité l'Ecosse avec ma famille pour fêter le mariage d'un cousin avec une jeune Ecossaise.**

Mon cousin habite une ferme près de la frontière anglaise et j'ai trouvé le paysage très charmant mais les fermes étaient beaucoup plus petites que les fermes canadiennes! Après le mariage nous avons loué une voiture pour explorer le pays. D'abord mon père a eu des difficultés parce que les Ecossais roulent à gauche et aussi très vite. Nous avons quand même visité beaucoup de jolis villages et avons aussi fait un tour sur le Loch Ness. C'était magnifique. Nous avons logé dans de petits hôtels et j'ai remarqué qu'il y avait beaucoup de jeunes étrangers qui travaillaient dans les restaurants et dans les hôtels. Ils venaient de partout dans le monde et surtout de l'Australie. Mon seul regret c'est que papa a refusé de s'acheter un kilt. «Mes jambes sont trop courtes» a-t-il dit!

(3 minutes)

(t)   Question number three.

Another participant tells you about his work placement in Africa.

(m)   L'année dernière j'ai fait un stage professionnel en Afrique pour deux bonnes raisons: D'abord parce que c'est ma passion de travailler avec les gens et puis j'ai toujours voulu mieux connaître d'autres cultures.

Notre groupe est arrivé au village à 3 heures du matin après un trajet de sept heures en autobus. On était donc très fatigué et on s'est couché tout de suite. Le lendemain, la journée a commencé par une réunion d'accueil pour tous les participants. L'après-midi, j'ai rencontré mes collègues de travail et j'ai commencé mon stage dans un hôpital, ce qui était très intéressant mais aussi très fatigant.

J'ai logé chez une famille africaine, dont les parents m'ont traité comme leur fils. La mère était très bonne cuisinière et a préparé plein de spécialités africaines. Une visite de trois mois que je n'oublierai jamais, surtout le jour de Noël quand on a fait un barbecue sur la plage et dansé toute la nuit.

(3 minutes)

(t)   End of test.

Now look over your answers.

[END OF TRANSCRIPT]

[BLANK PAGE]

FOR OFFICIAL USE

Mark

X059/202

NATIONAL
QUALIFICATIONS
2006

TUESDAY, 16 MAY
10.30 AM – 11.00 AM

FRENCH
INTERMEDIATE 2
Listening

Fill in these boxes and read what is printed below.

Full name of centre

Town

Forename(s)

Surname

Date of birth
Day   Month   Year   Scottish candidate number   Number of seat

When you are told to do so, open your paper.

You will hear three items in French. You will hear each item twice, with an interval of one minute between playings, then you will have time to answer the questions about it before hearing the next item.

Write your answers, **in English**, in this book, in the appropriate spaces.

You may take notes as you are listening to the French, but only in this book.

You may **not** use a French dictionary.

You are not allowed to leave the examination room until the end of the test.

Before leaving the examination room you must give this book to the invigilator. If you do not, you may lose all the marks for this paper.

SCOTTISH
QUALIFICATIONS
AUTHORITY

©

Points

You are working on a building project in Canada.

1. Céline, one of the other participants, tells you about her home and school life in the North of Canada.

   (*a*) How far is it to the nearest school?

   1

   _____

   (*b*) What happens at the following times? Write **one** thing in each box.

   3

8.00 am	
7.00 am	
7.30 am	

   (*c*) Why are languages important to her?

   1

   _____

   (*d*) What housework does Céline do to help her mum? Mention any **two** things.

   2

   _____

   _____

   (*e*) What is the **only disadvantage** Céline mentions of having lessons on the Internet?

   1

   _____

   *   *   *   *   *

Points

2. Céline then goes on to tell you about a visit she made to Scotland.

(*a*) When did she visit Scotland?

1

_____

(*b*) Where exactly does her cousin live? Mention **two** things.

2

_____

_____

(*c*) Why did her dad have difficulties driving in Scotland? Mention any **one** thing.

1

_____

(*d*) What did Céline notice about the young people who worked in the restaurants and hotels? Mention any **one** thing.

1

_____

(*e*) Why would her father not buy a kilt?

1

_____

*   *   *   *   *

[Turn over for Question 3 on *Page four*

Points

3. Another participant tells you about his work placement in Africa.

(*a*) Why did he decide to do this work placement in Africa? Mention any **one** thing.

1

_____

(*b*) What does he tell you about the journey to the village? Mention any **two** things.

2

_____

_____

(*c*) Where did he work during his placement?

1

_____

(*d*) He tells you about the family he stayed with. What does he say about the mother? Mention any **one** thing.

1

_____

(*e*) Why will he never forget how they spent Christmas day? Mention any **one** thing.

1

_____

*   *   *   *   *

**Total (20 points)
= 20 marks**

[*END OF QUESTION PAPER*]

X059/204

NATIONAL
QUALIFICATIONS
2006

TUESDAY, 16 MAY
11.20 AM – 12.00 NOON

FRENCH
INTERMEDIATE 2
Writing

20 marks are allocated to this paper.

You may use a French dictionary.

SCOTTISH
QUALIFICATIONS
AUTHORITY

You are preparing an application for the job advertised below.

Employeur:	Le village de Saint Nolff—3500 habitants.
Poste:	Animateur/animatrice pour les 12-18 ans dans une colonie de vacances.
Profil:	Mettre en place des activités linguistiques pour adolescents. Assurer l'animation des enfants.
Renseignements:	

Pour plus de détails sur les horaires, le salaire, l'hébergement etc.

Contactez

M le Maire,
Place de Pédrejas de San Estéban,
56250 Saint Nolff.

To help you to write your application, you have been given the following checklist of information to give about yourself and to ask about the job:

- name, age, where you live
- leisure interests
- school/college career – subjects studied previously/being studied now
- reasons for application
- request for information about the job.

Make sure you deal with **all** of these points. You could also include the following information:

- any previous links with France or a French-speaking country
- work experience, if any.

You have also been given a way to start and finish this formal type of letter:

Formal opening to letter of application

Monsieur/Madame/Messieurs,

Suite à votre annonce, je me permets de poser ma candidature pour le poste d'. . .

Formal finish to letter of application

En espérant que ma demande retiendra votre attention, je vous prie d'accepter, Monsieur/Madame/Messieurs, l'expression de mes sentiments distingués.

Use all of the above to help you write the letter which should be 120–150 words, excluding the formal phrases you have been given. You may use a French dictionary.

[END OF QUESTION PAPER]

[BLANK PAGE]

FOR OFFICIAL USE

Mark

X059/201

NATIONAL
QUALIFICATIONS
2007

THURSDAY, 17 MAY
9.00 AM – 10.10 AM

FRENCH
INTERMEDIATE 2
Reading

Fill in these boxes and read what is printed below.

Full name of centre

Town

Forename(s)

Surname

Date of birth
Day Month Year   Scottish candidate number   Number of seat

When you are told to do so, open your paper and write your answers **in English** in the spaces provided.

You may use a French dictionary.

Before leaving the examination room you must give this book to the invigilator. If you do not, you may lose all the marks for this paper.

SCOTTISH
QUALIFICATIONS
AUTHORITY

Points

You would like to work in France and you look on the Internet for some information about jobs.

1. You see this job advert.

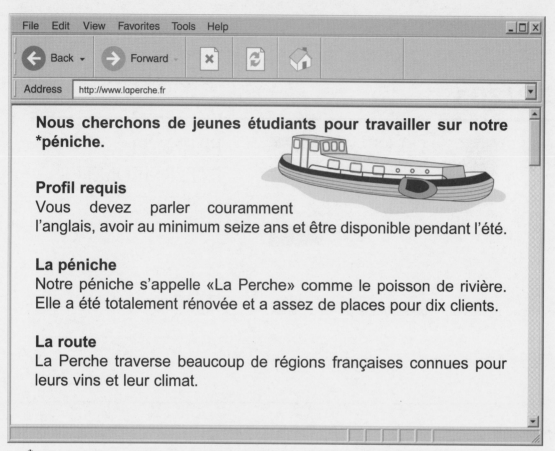

Nous cherchons de jeunes étudiants pour travailler sur notre *péniche.

Profil requis
Vous devez parler couramment l'anglais, avoir au minimum seize ans et être disponible pendant l'été.

La péniche
Notre péniche s'appelle «La Perche» comme le poisson de rivière. Elle a été totalement rénovée et a assez de places pour dix clients.

La route
La Perche traverse beaucoup de régions françaises connues pour leurs vins et leur climat.

*une péniche = barge/canal boat

(a) According to the title, what type of people should apply for this job?   **1**

_____

(b) What requirements must you have to be able to apply for the job? Mention any **two** things.   **2**

_____

_____

(c) Mention any **one** detail about the barge "La Perche".   **1**

_____

(d) The barge passes through many regions of France. What **two** things are they famous for?   **1**

_____

Points

2. You are interested in this job and you read on to find out more.

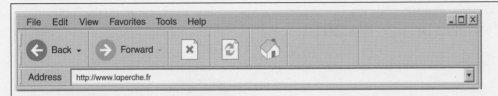

Vos tâches
Vous serez responsable du nettoyage des cabines et des visites guidées à chaque *escale.

Vos horaires
Vous travaillerez six heures par jour, cinq jours par semaine.

Les loisirs
Pendant votre temps libre vous pourrez descendre pour marcher le long du canal ou si vous préférez, vous pourrez rester à bord pour faire de la lecture.

L'hébergement et les repas
Vous partagerez votre cabine avec deux autres personnes. A bord il y a une petite cuisine toute équipée pour préparer les repas.

*une escale = port of call/stop

(a) Which **two** tasks will you be responsible for?　　　　　2

_____

_____

(b) How long will you work **per week**?　　　　　1

_____

(c) What can you do during your free time, if you get off the barge?　　　　　1

_____

(d) What details are you given about the facilities on board? Mention any **one** thing.　　　　　1

_____

[Turn over

DO NOT
WRITE I.
THIS
MARGI

Points

3. You read an article in a French magazine in which two young people give their views on the venue chosen for the Olympic Games of 2012.

Les Jeux Olympiques de 2012

Deux jeunes Parisiens donnent leur avis.

Farid — 21 ans

Moi je suis très content que Paris n'organise pas les Jeux Olympiques.

Les Jeux Olympiques coûtent cher car il faut construire des stades, de nouvelles routes et des logements pour les athlètes. De plus, les Jeux Olympiques créent plus de circulation dans la ville. Bon courage Londres.

Christine — 16 ans

Moi, au contraire, je suis triste que Paris n'organise pas les Jeux Olympiques.

Les Jeux Olympiques encouragent les jeunes à pratiquer un sport, créent de nombreux emplois et cela renforce l'amitié entre les pays participants.

Farid

(*a*) Farid says that the Olympic Games cost a lot of money. Why? Mention any **two** things.

2

_____

_____

(*b*) What other disadvantage does he mention?

1

_____

Christine

(*c*) Christine would have been happy for Paris to host the Olympic Games. Why? Mention any **two** things.

2

_____

_____

[Turn over for Question 4 on *Pages six, seven* and *eight*

4. You read another article about things that annoy people in today's society.

Ça m'énerve

Beaucoup de choses dans la société moderne améliorent notre vie de tous les jours, par exemple on peut acheter ses courses par Internet, communiquer avec ses amis par ordinateur et aller à l'étranger pour moins de cinq euros. Mais sommes-nous toujours satisfaits de ces changements?

Il paraît que non! Deux jeunes gens parlent de ce qui les énerve.

Sylvie — 20 ans

Dans notre société moderne la protection de l'environnement est une des choses dont on parle le plus, pourtant les gens continuent à utiliser leur voiture dans les centres-villes. **Et ça, ça m'énerve!**

Les gens ne veulent pas utiliser les bus car ils disent que les bus sont souvent surchargés, sales et en retard. Mais pourquoi ne pas aller en ville à pied ou en vélo? Par exemple mon père ne se déplace qu'en vélo pour aller au travail. Non seulement le vélo est un moyen de transport propre mais il permet aussi de faire de l'exercice.

Si on habite loin de son travail on peut toujours laisser sa voiture dans les grands parkings autour de la ville et puis prendre le métro. Dans ma ville, le centre est interdit aux voitures; il y a donc moins de bruit et les gens peuvent se promener sans danger.

Thomas — 16 ans

Aujourd'hui tout le monde utilise un téléphone portable n'importe où et n'importe quand. **Et ça, ça m'énerve!!**

Il est vrai que le téléphone portable peut être très utile en cas de panne de voiture ou en cas d'urgence médicale par exemple. Mais est-il vraiment nécessaire d'utiliser son téléphone dans un restaurant pour décrire ce que l'on mange ou au supermarché pour demander ce qu'il faut acheter?

Ce qui m'énerve le plus? C'est quand on sort avec des amis et qu'ils passent la soirée à envoyer des minis-messages au lieu de me parler.

De plus le téléphone portable devrait être interdit à l'école. La sonnerie des téléphones interrompt les cours et les élèves perdent donc leur concentration et par conséquent ils ne comprennent pas forcément la leçon.

Points

4. (continued)

(*a*) A lot of things improve our everyday life. Mention any **two** examples that are given.

2

_____

_____

Sylvie

(*b*) What annoys Sylvie in today's modern society?

1

_____

(*c*) According to Sylvie, why do people not want to use buses? Mention any **two** things.

2

_____

_____

(*d*) Her dad goes to work by bike. Why does Sylvie think that a bike is a good means of transport? Mention any **one** thing.

1

_____

(*e*) What does Sylvie suggest you do if you live far from your work?

2

_____

_____

(*f*) In the centre of Sylvie's town, cars are forbidden. Mention **one** advantage of this.

1

_____

_____

Thomas

(*g*) Mobile phones can be very useful. Mention any **one** example that Thomas gives.

1

_____

Points

4. (continued)

(*h*)   Thomas gives two examples of people using their mobile phones where it is not necessary.

In the grid below, write the reason why they use their phone in each place.

2

Place	Reason
Restaurant	
Supermarket	

(*i*)   What annoys Thomas most when he goes out with his friends?

1

_____

(*j*)   Why does Thomas think that mobile phones should be forbidden in schools? Mention any **two** things.

2

_____

_____

Total (30 points)

= 30 marks

[END OF QUESTION PAPER]

X059/203

NATIONAL
QUALIFICATIONS
2007

THURSDAY, 17 MAY
10.30 AM – 11.00 AM

FRENCH
INTERMEDIATE 2
Listening Transcript

This paper must not be seen by any candidate.

The material overleaf is provided for use in an emergency only (eg the recording or equipment proving faulty) or where permission has been given in advance by SQA for the material to be read to candidates with additional support needs. The material must be read exactly as printed.

SCOTTISH
QUALIFICATIONS
AUTHORITY

Instructions to reader(s):

For each item, read the English **once**, then read the French **twice**, with an interval of 1 minute between the two readings. On completion of the second reading, pause for the length of time indicated in brackets after each item, to allow the candidates to write their answers.

Where special arrangements have been agreed in advance to allow the reading of the material, those sections marked **(f)** should be read by a female speaker and those marked **(m)** by a male: those sections marked **(t)** should be read by the teacher.

(t) In the summer you are working on a barge in France.

Question number one.

While in France you meet Maryse who comes from Lyon. She tells you about her everyday life.

You now have one minute to study the question.

(f) Bonjour! Je m'appelle Maryse et j'habite à 5 kilomètres de Lyon avec mes parents et ma petite soeur. Je m'entends très bien avec mes parents mais ma petite soeur est très paresseuse et nous nous disputons tout le temps. Ma mère est infirmière et travaille tard, donc le soir je mets la table et je prépare le dîner. Ma mère me donne de l'argent de poche mais je veux gagner un peu plus d'argent parce que je veux aller en Espagne l'année prochaine. Donc, le week-end, je travaille comme serveuse dans un restaurant à Lyon. Ça me permet de mettre de l'argent sur mon compte en banque pour les vacances, d'acheter des vêtements et de sortir avec mes amis. Je trouve les petits boulots très utiles. Ça donne aux jeunes une première expérience du monde du travail et nous rend plus indépendants.

(*3 minutes*)

(t) Question number two.

Maryse goes on to tell you a little more about Lyon.

You now have one minute to study the question.

(f) Lyon est situé dans l'Est de la France et a un climat très variable. En été, par exemple, le matin il peut faire très chaud et puis à 3 heures il y a des orages. Lyon est très bien desservi par les transports avec un aéroport international à 25 kilomètres et on peut être à Paris en 2 heures avec le TGV, le train à grande vitesse qui est très confortable et rarement en retard. Comme Lyon est une ville universitaire, il y a beaucoup d'étudiants qui viennent y étudier la médecine, la politique et les langues étrangères par exemple. Lyon est aussi connu comme la capitale gastronomique française et bien manger et boire sont très importants pour les habitants. On peut y acheter de bons jambons et toutes sortes de fromage. On dit que les gens de Lyon sont froids et assez distants mais bien sûr je ne suis pas d'accord.

(*3 minutes*)

(t) **Question number three.**

You then meet Rodolphe who spent some time in Scotland as a French assistant.

You now have one minute to study the question.

(m) L'année dernière j'ai passé un an dans une école écossaise comme assistant de français. J'ai travaillé avec des petits groupes d'élèves âgés entre 11 et 17 ans. J'ai fait des cours sur la vie en France et le cinéma français.

Un des meilleurs moments de mon séjour en Ecosse était lorsque je suis allé dans le Nord de l'Ecosse avec l'école. On a logé dans une auberge de jeunesse qui était très propre et moi j'ai partagé une chambre avec un professeur d'histoire qui accompagnait le groupe. On passait les matinées à visiter des châteaux, des monuments célèbres et des distilleries de whisky. L'après-midi on faisait de belles promenades sur les plages et des randonnées en montagne. J'ai ainsi pu prendre énormément de photos. Le paysage était magnifique mais j'étais étonné par le manque d'arbres. Un des profs m'a expliqué qu'il n'y a pas beaucoup d'arbres car il y a trop de vent. Cela dit j'ai passé une année extraordinaire en Ecosse. J'ai amélioré mon anglais et j'ai rencontré des gens très sympathiques. J'espère y retourner un jour.

(3 minutes)

(t) **End of test.**

Now look over your answers.

[END OF TRANSCRIPT]

[BLANK PAGE]

FOR OFFICIAL USE

Mark

X059/202

NATIONAL
QUALIFICATIONS
2007

THURSDAY, 17 MAY
10.30 AM – 11.00 AM

FRENCH
INTERMEDIATE 2
Listening

Fill in these boxes and read what is printed below.

Full name of centre

Town

Forename(s)

Surname

Date of birth
Day Month Year

Scottish candidate number

Number of seat

When you are told to do so, open your paper.

You will hear three items in French. **Before you hear each item, you will have one minute to study the question.** You will hear each item twice, with an interval of one minute between playings, then you will have time to answer the questions about it before hearing the next item.

Write your answers, **in English**, in this book, in the appropriate spaces.

You may take notes as you are listening to the French, but only in this book.

You may **not** use a French dictionary.

You are not allowed to leave the examination room until the end of the test.

Before leaving the examination room you must give this book to the invigilator. If you do not, you may lose all the marks for this paper.

SCOTTISH
QUALIFICATIONS
AUTHORITY

Points

DO NOT
WRITE IN
THIS
MARGIN

In the summer you are working on a barge in France.

1.   While in France you meet Maryse who comes from Lyon. She tells you about her everyday life.

(*a*)   How far away from Lyon does Maryse live?   **1**

_____

(*b*)   What does Maryse say about her little sister? Mention any **one** thing.   **1**

_____

(*c*)   What is Maryse's mother's job?   **1**

_____

(*d*)   How does Maryse help out in the house? Mention any **one** thing.   **1**

_____

(*e*)   Which job does Maryse do at the weekend to earn some extra money?   **1**

_____

(*f*)   What does she do with the money she earns from her job? Mention any **two** things.   **2**

_____

_____

(*g*)   Why does Maryse think part-time jobs are useful for young people? Mention any **one** thing.   **1**

_____

*   *   *   *   *

Points

2. Maryse goes on to tell you a little more about Lyon.

(*a*) Where exactly is Lyon situated?   **1**

_____

(*b*) The weather in Lyon is very variable in the summer. Complete the
following sentence.

In the morning the weather can be _____ but by 3 pm it

can be _____ .   **1**

(*c*) How long does it take to go from Lyon to Paris by train?   **1**

_____

(*d*) What subjects can students study at the University of Lyon? Mention
any **two**.   **2**

_____

_____

(*e*) Eating and drinking are very important to the people of Lyon. Name
the **two** items of food that are mentioned.   **1**

_____

*   *   *   *   *

[Turn over for Question 3 on *Page four*

Points

3. You then meet Rodolphe who spent some time in Scotland as a French assistant.

(*a*) Complete the sentence.

Rodolphe taught pupils between the ages of _____ and _____ .   **1**

(*b*) What did Rodolphe teach in his lessons? Mention any **one** thing.   **1**

_____

(*c*) Rodolphe went on a school trip to the north of Scotland. Where did he stay?   **1**

_____

(*d*) What did they visit in the morning? Mention any **one** thing.   **1**

_____

(*e*) What did they do in the afternoon? Mention any **one** thing.   **1**

_____

(*f*) He was surprised by the lack of trees. What reason did a teacher give him for this?   **1**

_____

*   *   *   *   *

**Total (20 points)
= 20 marks**

[*END OF QUESTION PAPER*]

X059/204

NATIONAL
QUALIFICATIONS
2007

THURSDAY, 17 MAY
11.20 AM – 12.00 NOON

FRENCH
INTERMEDIATE 2
Writing

20 marks are allocated to this paper.

You may use a French dictionary.

SCOTTISH
QUALIFICATIONS
AUTHORITY

©

You are preparing an application for the job advertised below.

Employeur:	Hôtel les Mélèzes
Poste:	Réceptionniste
Profil:	Accueillir les clients et les renseigner sur la ville et la région. Une connaissance de la langue française est indispensable.

Renseignements:

Pour plus de détails sur les horaires, le salaire, l'hébergement etc.

Contactez

Mme Dupont,
Hôtel les Mélèzes,
Tignes.

To help you to write your application, you have been given the following checklist of information to give about yourself and to ask about the job:

- name, age, where you live
- leisure interests
- school/college career – subjects studied previously/being studied now
- reasons for application
- request for information about the job.

Make sure you deal with **all** of these points. You could also include the following information:

- any previous links with France or a French-speaking country
- work experience, if any.

You have also been given a way to start and finish this formal type of letter:

Formal opening to letter of application

Monsieur/Madame/Messieurs,

Suite à votre annonce, je me permets de poser ma candidature pour le poste de . . .

Formal finish to letter of application

En espérant que ma demande retiendra votre attention, je vous prie d'accepter, Monsieur/Madame/Messieurs, l'expression de mes sentiments distingués.

Use all of the above to help you write **in French** the letter which should be 120–150 words, excluding the formal phrases you have been given. You may use a French dictionary.

[END OF QUESTION PAPER]

[BLANK PAGE]

FOR OFFICIAL USE

Mark

X059/201

NATIONAL
QUALIFICATIONS
2008

WEDNESDAY, 21 MAY
9.00 AM – 10.10 AM

FRENCH
INTERMEDIATE 2
Reading

Fill in these boxes and read what is printed below.

Full name of centre

Town

Forename(s)

Surname

Date of birth
Day   Month   Year   Scottish candidate number   Number of seat

When you are told to do so, open your paper and write your answers **in English** in the spaces provided.

You may use a French dictionary.

Before leaving the examination room you must give this book to the invigilator. If you do not, you may lose all the marks for this paper.

Question 4 is on fold-out pages 6, 7 and 8.

Points

1. You are looking for a job in a French speaking country and you find an Internet website for a company in Belgium.

Vous voulez travailler dans un environnement motivant et dynamique?

Nous recherchons des étudiant(e)s pour travailler comme
* jardiniers
* vendeurs/euses de glaces
* cuisiniers

Nous sommes une très grande compagnie avec sept parcs d'attractions en Europe et nous avons plus de quatre mille employés.

C'est l'endroit idéal pour toute la famille. Ce n'est pas cher. Le prix d'entrée inclut toutes les activités sauf les repas et les boissons.

(a) Which jobs are being advertised? Mention any **two**.　　2

_____

_____

(b) You are given information about the company. To what do the following numbers refer?　　2

7	
4000	

(c) What does the entry price include?　　1

_____

Points

2. You also find a blog where Jean-Paul, who has previously worked for the company, writes about his experiences.

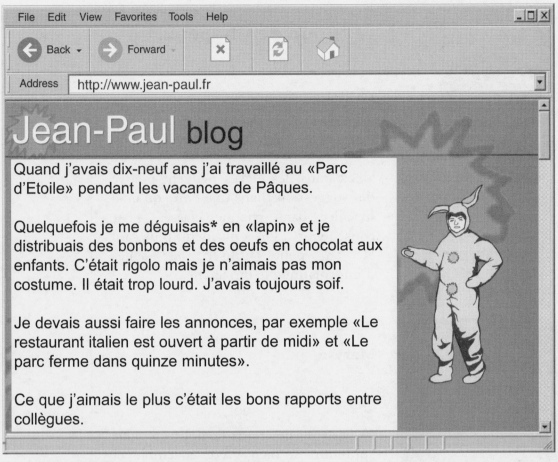

File   Edit   View   Favorites   Tools   Help

Back ▾   Forward   ✕   ↻   🏠

Address   http://www.jean-paul.fr

Jean-Paul blog

Quand j'avais dix-neuf ans j'ai travaillé au «Parc d'Etoile» pendant les vacances de Pâques.

Quelquefois je me déguisais* en «lapin» et je distribuais des bonbons et des oeufs en chocolat aux enfants. C'était rigolo mais je n'aimais pas mon costume. Il était trop lourd. J'avais toujours soif.

Je devais aussi faire les annonces, par exemple «Le restaurant italien est ouvert à partir de midi» et «Le parc ferme dans quinze minutes».

Ce que j'aimais le plus c'était les bons rapports entre collègues.

*Se déguiser = to dress up as

(a) When did Jean-Paul work at the "Parc d'Etoile"? Mention any **one** thing.

1

_____

(b) Sometimes, as part of his job, he wore a rabbit costume. What did he have to do? Mention any **one** thing.

1

_____

(c) What did he not like about his costume? Mention any **one** thing.

1

(d) He also had to make announcements. Give **one** example of this.

1

_____

(e) What did he like most about his work?

1

_____

Points

DO NOT
WRITE I
THIS
MARGIN

3. While working in Belgium you read a magazine article in which pupils write about their school.

Coup de Chapeau!*

Philippe

Chez nous, les élèves peuvent mettre des suggestions dans une boîte qu'on a installée dans chaque classe. Par conséquent : On a un menu plus sain et on peut utiliser les salles d'informatique le dimanche.

Maryse

Nous avons des cours de politesse pour apprendre à bien vivre ensemble et pour décourager la violence. Par exemple dans les bus on devrait laisser sa place à une personne âgée, dire bonjour au chauffeur et ne pas jeter son ticket par terre.

---

*Coup de Chapeau! = Great Idea!

(*a*) In Philippe's school the pupils have suggestion boxes. What changes have been made? Mention **two** things.

2

_____

_____

Points

3. (continued)

(*b*) In Maryse's school they give lessons in politeness. Why? Mention any **one** thing.

1

(*c*) How should the pupils behave on buses? Mention any **two** things.

2

[Turn over for Question 4 on *Pages six, seven* and *eight*

4. You read an article about voluntary work in the magazine.

Comment aider les animaux ou les gens moins chanceux que vous ?

Il y a des milliers de façons d'être bénévole*. Entraîner une équipe de foot, travailler avec les animaux malades ou visiter les personnes handicapées etc. En plus de la satisfaction, le bénévolat* vous apporte une première expérience dans le monde du travail.

Deux jeunes gens parlent de ce qu'ils font en tant que bénévoles.

Yannick

Moi depuis tout petit, j'ai toujours voulu un chien mais ma mère était contre. Elle disait toujours — qui va promener le chien quand il pleut? Où va-t-on laisser le chien lorsqu'on part en vacances?

Donc j'ai décidé d'adopter un chien. Chaque mois j'envoie sept euros qui payent son logement et sa nourriture. En retour je reçois des cartes d'anniversaire et des autocollants, c'est génial. Et puis un jour j'ai lu un article dans le journal qui demandait des volontaires pour travailler avec les animaux abandonnés. J'y travaille donc depuis dix ans maintenant. On s'occupe d'oiseaux, de chats, de cobayes, de chiens etc. On leur donne à manger, nettoie leur cage et joue avec eux. En ce moment je suis à l'université pour faire des études de vétérinaire pour pouvoir un jour soigner les animaux.

Aisha

Il y a deux ans j'ai fait un échange scolaire au Mali*. J'étais bouleversée par la pauvreté de ce pays. Il n'y avait pas d'eau courante, les enfants étaient dans des classes de cinquante élèves et beaucoup de gens étaient malades car il n'y avait pas beaucoup de docteurs.

En rentrant en France, j'ai décidé d'être bénévole pour l'UNICEF*. On fait beaucoup de choses comme vendre des produits Unicef dans les grandes villes de France et on organise aussi des spectacles et des événements sportifs. L'argent collecté aide à construire des hôpitaux, nourrir les enfants et créer des écoles dans les villages.

De plus les élèves de mon lycée envoient des vêtements, des livres et des jouets aux enfants maliens. L'année prochaine je vais aller à la fac pour étudier la médecine car j'aimerais être médecin dans le Tiers Monde.

---

* **bénévole** = a volunteer   *le **bénévolat** = voluntary work

* **Mali** = a country in Africa   * **UNICEF** = a fund-raising organisation for children

DO NOT
WRITE IN
THIS
MARGIN

Points

4. (continued)

(*a*)   This article gives you some examples of voluntary work. Mention any **two**.

2

_____

_____

(*b*)   Apart from satisfaction, what other benefit will voluntary work bring you?

1

_____

Yannick talks about his love for animals.

(*c*)   Yannick's mum was against having a dog. What did she always say? Mention any **one** thing.

1

_____

(*d*)   Yannick pays seven euros to adopt a dog. What does this money pay for? Mention any **one** thing.

1

_____

(*e*)   What does Yannick receive in return from his adopted dog? Mention any **one** thing.

1

_____

(*f*)   How long has Yannick been working with animals which have been abandoned?

1

_____

(*g*)   Mention any **two** things he has to do for the abandoned animals.

2

_____

_____

Points

DO N
WRIT
THI
MARC

4. (continued)

Aisha talks about her visit to Mali, a country in Africa.

(*h*) Aisha was upset by the poverty in Mali. Mention any **two** examples
she gives.

2

_____

_____

(*i*) What does UNICEF do to raise money? Mention any **one** thing.

1

_____

_____

(*j*) What is the money collected by UNICEF used for? Mention any **two**
things.

2

_____

_____

(*k*) How do the pupils in Aisha's school help the children in Mali?
Mention any **one** thing.

1

_____

Total (30 points)

= 30 marks

[END OF QUESTION PAPER]

X059/203

NATIONAL
QUALIFICATIONS
2008

WEDNESDAY, 21 MAY
10.30 AM – 11.00 AM

FRENCH
INTERMEDIATE 2
Listening Transcript

This paper must not be seen by any candidate.

The material overleaf is provided for use in an emergency only (eg the recording or equipment proving faulty) or where permission has been given in advance by SQA for the material to be read to candidates with additional support needs. The material must be read exactly as printed.

Instructions to reader(s):

For each item, read the English **once**, then read the French **twice**, with an interval of 1 minute between the two readings. On completion of the second reading, pause for the length of time indicated in brackets after each item, to allow the candidates to write their answers.

Where special arrangements have been agreed in advance to allow the reading of the material, those sections marked **(f)** should be read by a female speaker and those marked **(m)** by a male: those sections marked **(t)** should be read by the teacher.

(t)   Question number one.

You have arrived in Belgium to work in an amusement park.

You now have one minute to study the question.

(f)   Bonsoir et bienvenue en Belgique. Je m'appelle Michelle Durand D-U-R-A-N-D et je suis la responsable du personnel. C'est moi que vous contactez si vous avez des questions. Comme vous savez vous travaillerez 35 heures par semaine avec deux jours de congé. Vous recevrez 8 euros de l'heure avec l'hébergement et les repas compris. Vous partagerez un chalet à trois chambres avec une petite cuisine qui est très pratique pour préparer le petit déjeuner. Quant au déjeuner et au dîner il y a une cantine pour le personnel près de la sortie du parc. On vous fournit aussi votre uniforme: une casquette rouge avec le nom du parc, un tee-shirt jaune et un pantalon noir. Nous fournissons même la crème solaire. Nous commençons la formation demain. Alors: Bonsoir et dormez bien.

(3 minutes)

(t)   Question number two.

Your staff meeting continues the following morning.

You now have one minute to study the question.

(f)   Bonjour tout le monde. J'espère que vous avez bien dormi. Aujourd'hui vous allez d'abord vous présenter au groupe pour mieux vous connaître. Ici on parle toujours en français car nous sommes de quinze nationalités différentes. Maintenant je vous explique les règlements du parc. Vous devez toujours arriver à l'heure pour commencer le travail et il est interdit de boire de l'alcool ou de fumer les jours de travail. Cet après-midi vous êtes libres pour explorer le parc. Il fait très beau aujourd'hui et je vous recommande donc d'aller voir notre grande piscine olympique. Ce soir vous pouvez visiter la ville voisine et aller en boîte de nuit ou faire les magasins. Les bus partent de l'entrée du parc toutes les demi-heures jusqu'à une heure du matin.

(3 minutes)

(t) **Question number three.**

While working in Belgium you meet a colleague, Robert, who comes from Martinique. He tells you a bit about himself, where he has been, and his native country.

You now have one minute to study the question.

(m) Bonjour, je m'appelle Robert et je viens de la Martinique. L'année prochaine je vais à l'université afin d'étudier les mathématiques. Mais d'abord je fais le tour du monde. J'ai déjà passé trois mois en Australie pour perfectionner mon anglais. Là j'ai travaillé dans une ferme. J'ai beaucoup aimé les animaux bizarres et les gens qui étaient toujours souriants. Ce que je n'aimais pas c'était les insectes dans les salles de bains et les serpents sous les lits! Je suis en Belgique depuis un mois et je la trouve bien différente de la Martinique. D'abord, la Martinique est une île montagneuse. Puis nous mangeons beaucoup plus de fruits et de légumes que les Belges. Tu veux me rendre visite en Martinique? Tu pourrais profiter du beau temps pour bronzer et aussi pour visiter les sites historiques.

(3 minutes)

(t) **End of test.**

Now look over your answers.

[END OF TRANSCRIPT]

[BLANK PAGE]

FOR OFFICIAL USE

Mark

X059/202

NATIONAL
QUALIFICATIONS
2008

WEDNESDAY, 21 MAY
10.30 AM – 11.00 AM

FRENCH
INTERMEDIATE 2
Listening

Fill in these boxes and read what is printed below.

Full name of centre

Town

Forename(s)

Surname

Date of birth
Day Month Year   Scottish candidate number   Number of seat

When you are told to do so, open your paper.

You will hear three items in French. **Before you hear each item, you will have one minute to study the question.** You will hear each item twice, with an interval of one minute between playings, then you will have time to answer the questions about it before hearing the next item.

Write your answers, **in English**, in this book, in the appropriate spaces.

You may take notes as you are listening to the French, but only in this book.

You may **not** use a French dictionary.

You are not allowed to leave the examination room until the end of the test.

Before leaving the examination room you must give this book to the invigilator. If you do not, you may lose all the marks for this paper.

Points

1. You have arrived in Belgium to work in an amusement park.

   (a) What is the name of the person who is responsible for staff?

   Tick **one** box.

   1

Michelle Dupont	
Michelle Durand	
Michelle Duchamp	

   (b) Why should you contact this person?

   1

   _____

   (c) How many hours will you work a week?

   1

   _____

   (d) How much will you earn an hour?

   1

   _____

   (e) What are you told about the chalet you will share? Mention any **one** thing.

   1

   _____

   (f) Where is the staff canteen?

   1

   _____

   (g) Describe your uniform. Mention any **two** things.

   2

   _____

   _____

   *   *   *   *   *

Points

2. Your staff meeting continues the following morning.

(*a*)   Why must everyone speak in French?   **1**

_____

(*b*)   Which rules must you follow at work?   Mention any **two** things.   **2**

_____

_____

_____

(*c*)   What is suggested you do in the afternoon?   Mention any **one** thing.   **1**

_____

(*d*)   Why might you visit the neighbouring town?   Mention any **one** thing.   **1**

_____

(*e*)   How often do the buses run?   **1**

_____

*   *   *   *   *

[Turn over for Question 3 on *Page four*

Points

3. While working in Belgium you meet a colleague, Robert, who comes from Martinique. He tells you a bit about himself, where he has been, and his native country.

(*a*) What is Robert going to study at university?

1

_____

(*b*) Why did he go to Australia? Mention any **one** thing.

1

_____

(*c*) What did he like about Australia? Mention any **one** thing.

1

_____

(*d*) What did he not like about Australia? Mention any **one** thing.

1

_____

(*e*) What does he tell you about Martinique? Mention any **one** thing.

1

_____

(*f*) Robert invites you to Martinique. What does he suggest you can do there? Mention any **one** thing.

1

_____

*   *   *   *   *

**Total (20 points)
= 20 marks**

[*END OF QUESTION PAPER*]

X059/204

NATIONAL
QUALIFICATIONS
2008

WEDNESDAY, 21 MAY
11.20 AM – 12.00 NOON

FRENCH
INTERMEDIATE 2
Writing

20 marks are allocated to this paper.

You may use a French dictionary.

You are preparing an application for the job advertised below.

Titre du poste:	Guide touristique
Description de l'offre:	Guide touristique en France et en Europe de l'Ouest. Hébergement en France. Le/La candidat(e) devra avoir une bonne présentation et le sens des responsabilités. Langues étrangères obligatoires.

To help you to write your application, you have been given the following checklist of information to give about yourself and to ask about the job:

- name, age, where you live
- leisure interests
- school/college career – subjects studied previously/being studied now
- reasons for application
- request for information about the job.

Make sure you deal with **all** of these points. You could also include the following information:

- any previous links with France or a French-speaking country
- work experience, if any.

You have also been given a way to start and finish this formal type of letter:

Formal opening to letter of application

Monsieur/Madame/Messieurs,

Suite à votre annonce, je me permets de poser ma candidature pour le poste de . . .

Formal finish to letter of application

En espérant que ma demande retiendra votre attention, je vous prie d'accepter, Monsieur/Madame/Messieurs, l'expression de mes sentiments distingués.

Use all of the above to help you write **in French** the letter which should be 120–150 words, excluding the formal phrases you have been given. You may use a French dictionary.

[END OF QUESTION PAPER]

[BLANK PAGE]

[BLANK PAGE]

[BLANK PAGE]

[BLANK PAGE]

[BLANK PAGE]

[BLANK PAGE]